Then one day, in the little town of Nazareth, an angel came to visit a young woman named Mary. The angel said that God had chosen her to be the mother of the king. She must call him Jesus.

Mary's husband-to-be, Joseph, agreed to look after Mary and her baby. On the night Jesus was born, in a stable in Bethlehem, angels sang for joy. Wise men saw a star in the sky and knew it was a sign that a baby king had been born. They came to give him gifts.

An angel told Mary that she was to be the mother of Jesus, God's king.

When Jesus was growing up, no one seemed to notice anything special about him. At home in Nazareth, Joseph taught Jesus to be a carpenter.

Then one day Jesus left this work and began telling people about God. He chose twelve people to be his friends and his disciples. He said he needed them to help him in the work of teaching people how to live as God's friends – part of God's kingdom.

As a grown man, Jesus began to tell people about God.

Crowds of people came to listen.

'God wants you to love one another,' Jesus told them. 'You must even love your enemies. Pray for them and ask God to bless them.'

'Forgive one another,' Jesus told them. 'Then God will forgive you the things you do wrong.'

'Always remember to pray to God,' Jesus told them. 'Speak to God as if you were speaking to a loving father.'

Jesus told people to love God
and to love one another.

The people also came because Jesus could perform miracles. With just a touch he could make people well. Jesus healed blind people, and they could see. He cured lame people, and they could walk. He touched people with all kinds of illnesses and made them completely better.

Jesus worked miracles that made people well.

Jesus did other miracles as well.

One day more than 5000 people sat all day listening to Jesus. They grew very hungry. The only food anyone had was  five loaves and two fishes. Jesus said a prayer of thanks to God and asked his friends to share the food with the crowd. It was enough for everyone!

One night Jesus got into a boat with his friends to sail to the other side of a lake. A wild storm blew up and the friends were terrified. Jesus stood up and told the wind to be quiet. He told the waves to be still. At once the storm ended.

Jesus worked miracles that showed he had power from God.

Jesus also told stories.

'A shepherd had 100 sheep. One day he noticed that one was missing.

'He left the 99 and went to find the one that was lost. At last he found it. He picked it up and carried it home.

'Then he called his friends. "Come and let's be happy together," he said. "I have found my lost sheep."

'God is like that shepherd,' said Jesus.

Jesus told stories to help people understand that God loves them.

Jesus also told this story:

'A man was going on a journey. As he walked, robbers came and beat him up. They left him lying in the road.

'A temple priest came by. He saw the man but did not stop. He hurried by.

'A temple helper came by. He came closer to have a look. Then he hurried by.

'A foreigner came by, a Samaritan. He took the man to an inn. He made sure the man was looked after till he was better.

'You should be kind to others in the same way,' Jesus said to his listeners.

Jesus told stories to help people understand how to treat others.

Many people liked Jesus. They believed that the things he said were true.

One day, when Jesus and his friends were travelling to the big city of Jerusalem, the crowds began to cheer.

'Here comes God's special king,' they said. They cut branches from palm trees and waved them like flags.

Other people did not like Jesus. Many priests and religious teachers did not like him. 'Jesus is a troublemaker,' they whispered. 'We must get rid of him.'

Jesus did only good things,
but some people hated him.

Jesus knew what they were thinking. A few days later he shared bread and wine with his friends. At the meal he warned them that he was going to die.

Jesus was right. He had done no wrong, but people told lies about him. The very next day, a Friday, Jesus was put to death – crucified.

Some of his friends laid his body in a tomb like a cave and rolled the stone door shut.

Jesus was put to death
as if he had done bad things.

Early on the Sunday morning some friends of Jesus went to the tomb. They found the door open. They found the cave empty.

Soon after Jesus' friends had amazing news to tell: they had seen Jesus alive!

God had raised Jesus to life –
to show that his message was true,
to show that death was not the end.

Jesus rose to life again.

Forty days later Jesus' friends saw him go up to heaven. God made them brave and strong to go and tell the news about Jesus to all the world.

The news is that everyone must love one another, just as God loves us.

The news is that Jesus has opened the door to heaven, where those who love God are part of God's kingdom.

Jesus opened the way to heaven.